POLITICS THROUGH a LOCAL INTRANET

introduction to civic thinking

www.publicdom.net
publicdombooks@gmail.com

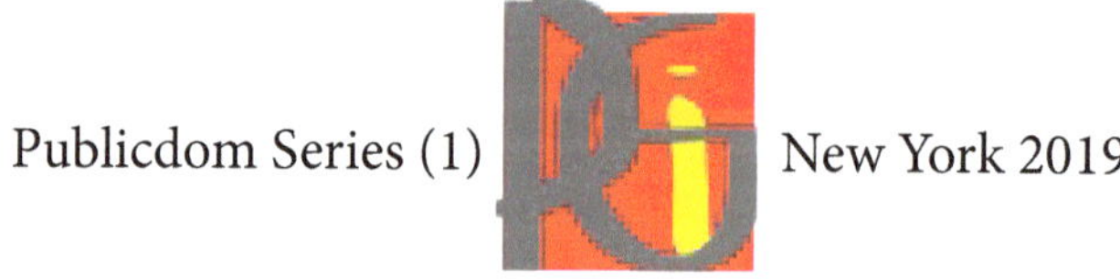

Publicdom Series (1)   New York 2019

CONTENT

Preface — TO THE SECOND EDITION

Your intelligence tells you that to paint your picture of the world more freely, there has to be a mechanism in which everyone else can take part in the painting. My intention here is to focus rather on the mechanism in creating our imminent world before we can co-paint it.

The massive, disagreements, personal disconnections and the mutually excluding arguments on the public level come from a gross misconception of a coherent environment. Think about it. Can one goal be better than many? Can one leader pursue different goals? How far does the voters' advancement have to go to embrace structural autonomies on the community level?

Democracy by definition has diverse interests at its core and potentially different ways of doing business. As the interests are real, they call for a realistic approach. What're the requirements? Is the task of democratization too big? If this were the case, this book would never be written.

The existing municipal estates are owned by the public as a common good—an ideal concept to build upon. The common interest, with the potential of full public involvement invokes meaning. A one share of municipality estate per respective citizen delivers it.

The one share rule of local municipalities is the shortest way to have a real integrated interest without starting from scratch. Note that shared ownership is the flagship of corporations, of course not the one share per co-owner promoted here.

NY 2019

aggrandizing socioeconomic life
takes nothing more than tapping
into the unlimited potential
participatory democracy has to offer,
while uniting political careers with
the public expectations to participate

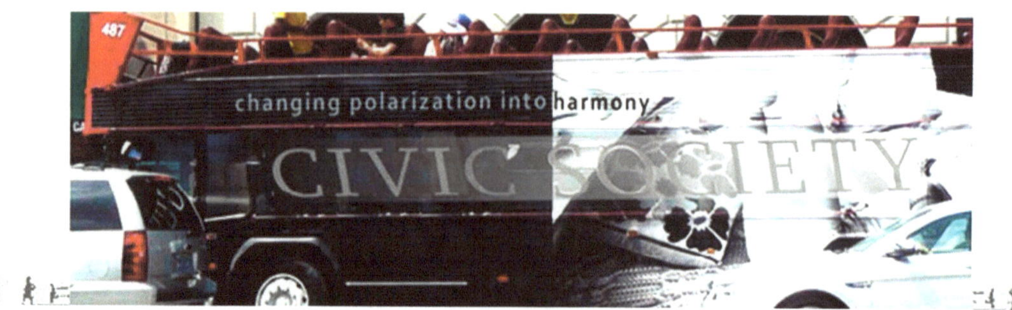

1 QUO VADIS

Term "collective consciousness" constitutes a palette of social metaphors with feelings sprang from personal foresight and related information, therefore "collective political consciousness" must be even more remote – why? Isn't it everybody's business. My thoughts have been evolving around issues like this enough, to sense what it takes for the society to be on the same page. The purpose of this introduction to social thinking is to give you the reader the material as a presentation.

Heritage of social sciences has always been a collection of interpretations and analyses of assorted social attitudes. As social evolution has been lead by narrow interests, so seeking conceptual answers must avoid the adjective "narrow."

My initial instinct led me in the direction taken everyone else in the field: to develop better and more convincing arguments for circulated issues needed to influence people. Arguments seldom work outside and can be withheld, for the most part. In their private life, people act upon their convictions and will support only trends that agree with them. The simple fact puts all politically tented discussions we encountered into question. Polemics sprang from, and news we cannot do anything about it – why? Can the news have practical meaning?

The foundation of social construct could have citizens' plug-ins – do away with citizenry as outsiders: to acknowledge the state of technology for establishing their presence.

The intent to be counted exists more or less consciously among the citizenry and are valid for practical, local reasons. What pushes polarization? The political metaphors of "the left" and "the right" are individuals' desire to function in a healthy mental state. Why can't they? The thing to acknowledge here is the simplicity to solve the incompatibility problem. You don't interfere with what already exists. By doing so, you are giving yourself the right to introduce things that are better.

Collective consciousness remains an enigmatic phenomenon, and the diversity it represents is far from authority's concerns. The path to knowing ourselves is the domain of a more controlled environment. The tool presented here for this purpose is called Municipal Citizen Account. To use its potential is to replace any politically dividing factors for more inclusive approaches.

I am concerned with the massive potential an integrated social network has (or will have) in a controlled environment as a bridge between the citizen, the representative and the local administration. Do not be discouraged by the word "local." Comprehensive systems – let's remember – have no gaps in it. Universality starts locally when participation is physically accessible to you.

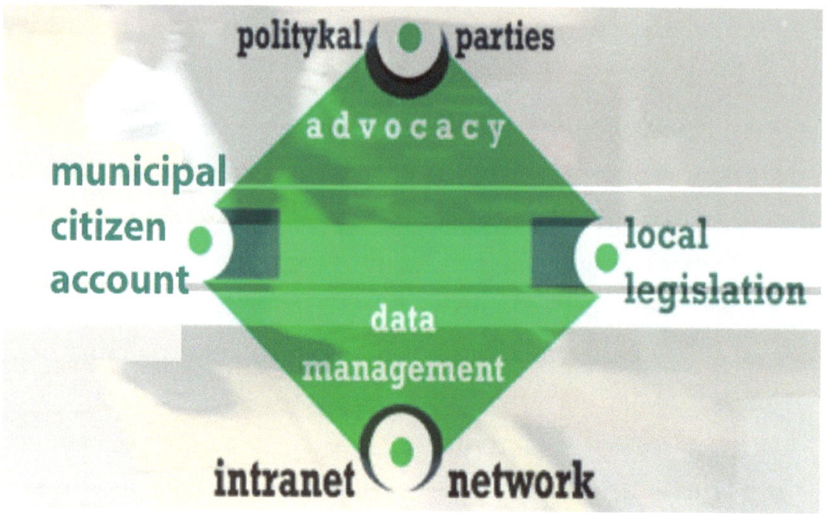

2 PUBLIC GOVERNMENT INTEGRATION

Let me say where I am going. I am going beyond the concept of an open government that emphasizes transparency and petitioning. The task is to comprehend the concept of publicly verifiable outcomes where cooperation takes place of polarization. There cannot be a valid political framework that favors one legitimate interest over another, where standard election practices only honor the most popular orientation and result in a massive chunk of no-luck votes among the underrepresented population. Local elections have distinct features from national ones. Among them the possibility of electing local leaders committed to acting on the direct support and approval of the community. All sustainable supports need to be evaluated, not eliminated. The political strength or weakness of local administration comes from the level of political support and the community's ability to generate it.

Though political writings are personal, one ought to go beyond one's subjectivity when the broader perspective is called for. The same goes for you, the reader. Sure you want to see everything from your perspective. This won't change. My point is that a valid perspective can be materialized along other valid perspectives simultaneously. Development suffers when fragmented.

The permanent feature in human behavior is the response to incentives. Therefore political apparatus needs to have a bright future in public service. When diverse interests are the objectives, different skills are needed to obtain results aligned with the expectations. We all know where we stand, but we most likely do not know how a political platform accommodating different orientations would work, specifically in the area of decision making. When two fights, the third wins. We may realize why no social trends could ever stand exclusively on its own ending the ever-present election time bickery—with not many results.

What sounds unfamiliar to us in the majority-minority culture is the concept of coordination needed to stay afloat—both. Political diversity is not a lottery choosing this or that, but the need for continuous involvement. Wealth and poverty are not diversities, nor is ethnicity in the collective era. Diversities emerge through self-classification and develop through a mechanism that favors them. So, tangible, workable cooperation between the general population and the administration is needed to cross the limitations.

Politics can be a love affair between the local government and the community it serves. The beauty is that only one element needs to be moved toward local citizenry: ratification of legislation. Publicly conscious leaders will gain competence with the support for the population-centered agenda recorded There is a law preventing administration from engaging in campaigns, but no law preventing communities and the administration from developing policies together. The network-strong community as a lobbyist?

In this book, having no model to draw from, I struggled with the terminology related to the civic society whose diversified interests must involve a realistic and adequate approach. The underlying meaning of public–government integration must not be strange to politicians whose rhetoric operates in that mode daily. Using ideas of democracy in the selective mode will be extremely rare in participatory democracy.

I will touch upon the public–private relationship in general as equal entireties. Massages of autonomy for the sectors, less interference with one another's growth has a hard time getting through due to the misconception of ownership. Ultimately, it is the voters' role and privilege to work in the sectors economically sound – shaped by their choices. In the following chapters, I will tackle the logical construct of choices and decisions in a participatory setting. The writing is not commissioned, allowing me to focus on the content interest-neutral.

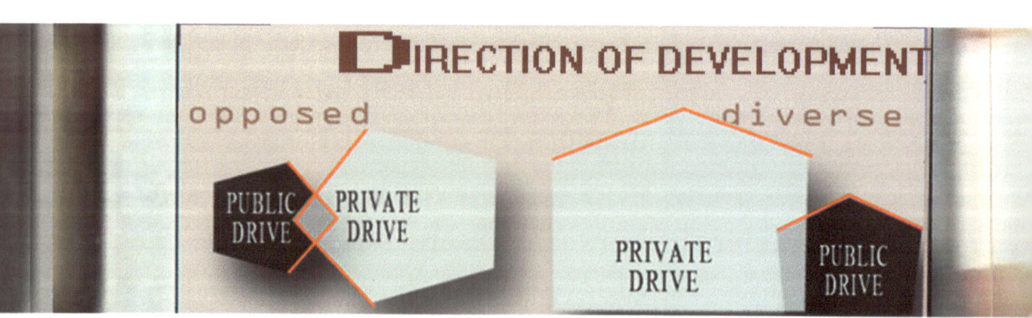

Participation implies an act of belonging. I am arguing for ways to go beyond social discrepancies, promoting approaches that are not on the public radar yet. The local population is more than a company or corporation, and in a public sense, we exist in disarray on any organizational level.

The inevitability of new technologies that significantly enable participation is not in doubt. Ambivalence seems to be a common occurrence in the entire spectrum of social communication, probably owing to too many passengers depending on traveling in the old wagon. Better public vehicles are needed to bring the public–government communication to a personal dashboard. Electronic democracy has yet to reach the preliminary blueprint stage.

The book subscribes to the idea that constructiveness operated by criticism does not seal well. It advocates following the widespread practices based on creating a set of stimuli for political factors, to make them predictable.

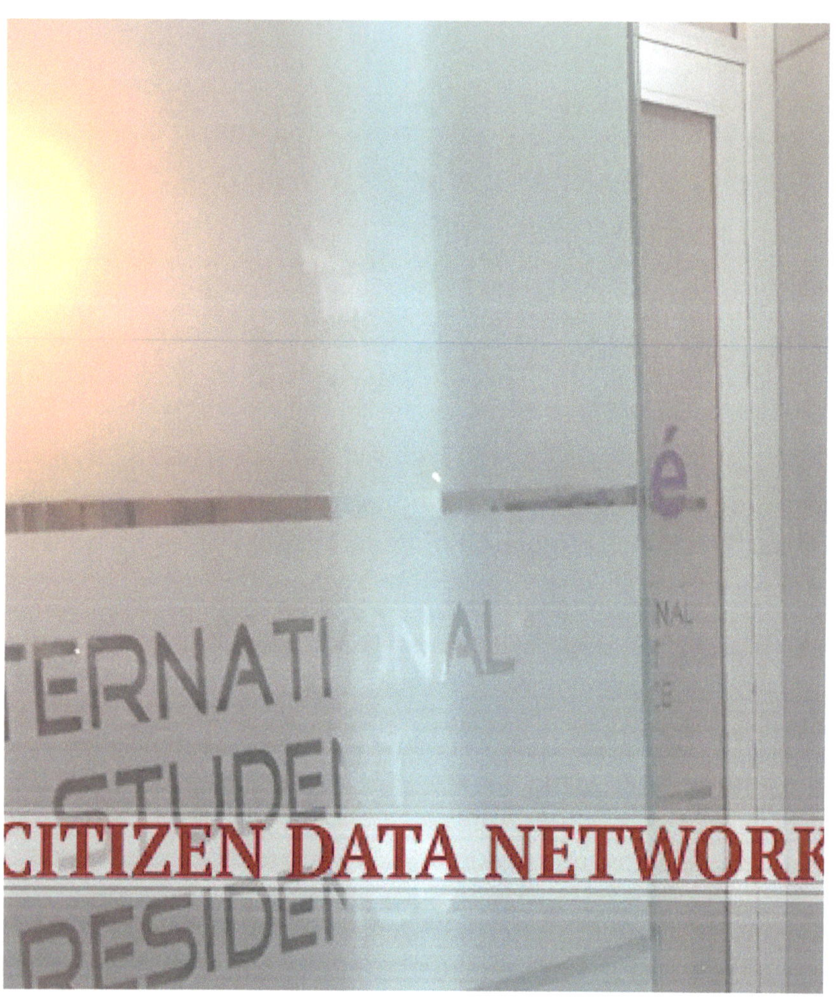
é
NAL
TERNATI NAL
STUDE
CITIZEN DATA NETWORK
RESIDE

3 VOTER CONTACT POINT

Subscribing to a hierarchical model in public relations delays the possibility of social scale communication and cooperation. This is one of my reasons for writing this book, thanks to the fact that advanced participation in the electronic era is for many a real possibility.

So what is the reality of running the public–government integration, and what shortcut on the functioning path should the public and aspiring politicians know about? The flow of relative data needs a container.

There is a saying that when things are too complicated and unfamiliar, it is better to simplify them to avoid confusion. The fact that legislation is written with the decision-making body in mind implies the need for voters to help local leaders keep the legislation on track. Having a public interest in public hands is in the spirit of the Constitution; to have it in selective hands is no longer necessary in the electronic era. Improving the mechanism of public effectiveness is the very purpose of living democracy, and by extension, the main argument for the public–government integration.

Municipal Citizen Account

Offering legislation for public ratification is an advanced business that goes beyond the concept presented in this chapter. Democratization processes preclude any certain development path, meaning that interconnectivity may develop in each community (the affluent and the run-down) independently, but be open to various adaptations by other municipalities. All levels of administration have public interest as a primary focus and therefore have a vital interest in obtaining the data-created knowledge.

It is understood low turnouts locally come from lousy organizing. Municipal Citizen Accounts are universal because the connection may supply functionality to elections, referendum, ballots, polls, information bulletins and similar. The manner of the public business led in public view should be network implemented.

To turn judgment into knowledge, the systematized public data are accessible on the local governmental network. This solution enables all users to draw upon it, guaranteeing the local administration's legislative body access to verified data. No one needs to wave signs on the streets for the evening news when effective mechanisms are available. Do not be discouraged by the lack of such a model; policies change as circumstances change. Therefore, public support is the building block of political integration, being potentially the prime currency in activating the interest in having politically inclusive lives through the community's might.

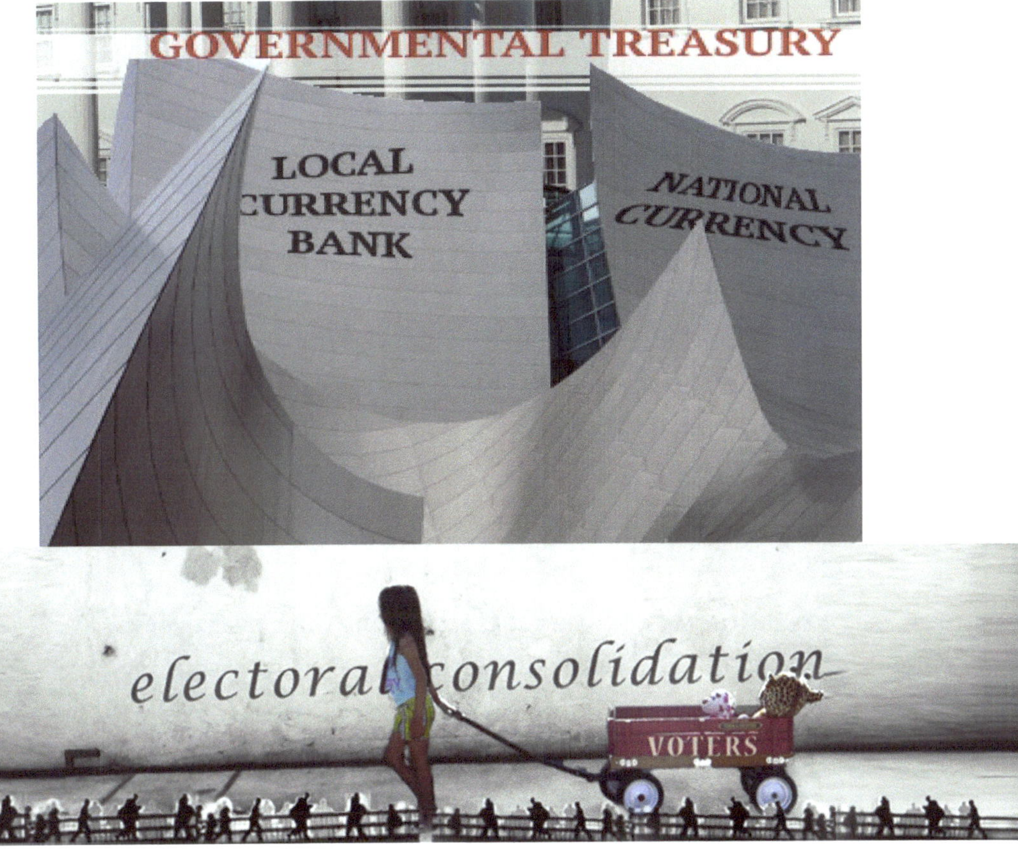

GOVERNMENTAL TREASURY
LOCAL CURRENCY BANK
NATIONAL CURRENCY
electoral consolidation
VOTERS

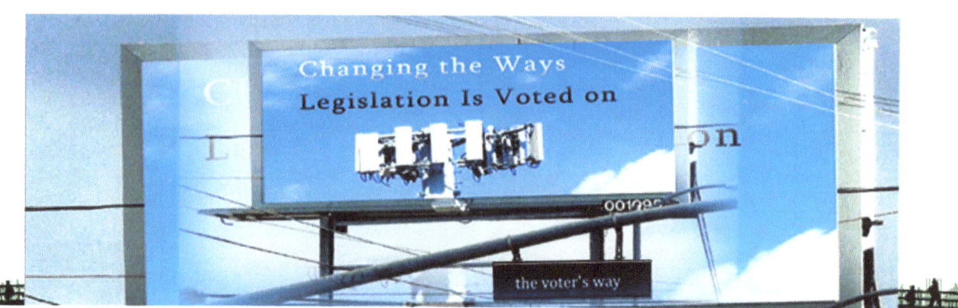

4 UPGRADING THE VOTER ROLE

Political representation has the potential to be the most strategic profession in the public realm; more like executive advisers if you will. Well, there always going to be a counterargument. A representative that operates on public data in the democratic setting tends to be more to the point than the one operating on judgments. Evolving on data is a striking proposition in which the platform for public feedback doesn't need to be from a science fiction scene.

Polarization stays in direct conflict with the principle of universal rights to freedom and prosperity through democratic means. Can the origins of paradoxes be traced? Stepping out from the snag of systematic limitations that prevents too many developments from taking place (note the plurality) is to see the big picture of physical disconnection from regulating and conditioning public life. Mentioning superficiality between the political majority and minority should surprise no one. The electoral rule of the alternating majority-gimmick and minority-pushback seems to have just another overlooked and self-inflicted attribute of a trap.

Though the labels change depending on the voting outcomes, the orientation on a deeper level stays the same with everyone. One thing leads to the other. To stay in public interest at large is to remain in political consideration before and after the election, and go where the division doesn't allow: toward limited autonomy under political contracts.

On the surface, such variety appears to be a complication. But we can assume people are eager to benefit from an environment that is not confrontational. A politics selectivity might be gradually reduced as participation helps to gain experience in approaching to challenges.

The political metaphors of "the left" and "the right" is the desire of the individuals to function in harmony with their characters. The thing to acknowledge is the simplicity to solve the incompatibility problem. The logic of collective interest may dictate more straightforward solutions in cases having sufficient backing. The gravity of the vote (as the political currency) to attract the interest of aspiring politicians is the best asset the public can have. Publicly discussed participatory democracy will catch the attention of candidates.

Citizens working on the market in the existing sectors, will jointly co-owned local municipality estate. This endeavor will produce a direct experience in new public coexistence, creating social harmony driven by having the rule of equal share in the business. This may seem idealistic but can become a reality once the picture of public support for sharing expressed locally starts to influence other aspects of public life.

DEBATE + PLATFORM

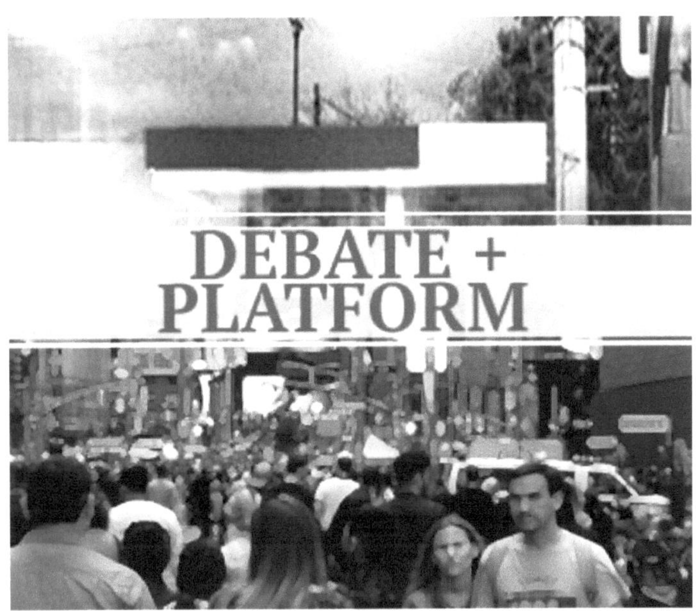

social springboard with the municipal joint venture

5 INTRANET APPROACH

A safe, reliable network for streaming public data is the promise of the path to socio-political awakening. To have a political profession up to the standard people view other professions requires the right means of passing the knowledge. To ensure administration quality, all aspect of public existence ought to be integrated. It is everybody's business including the representatives in key positions. Local networking is the long overdue effort of bridging the local administration, representatives and their constituency into the public realm. The flow of formal and informal content is needed for improving knowledge about political undertakings. You cannot interview members of community one by one: you have to have a system in place to gutter and process information at once. Working with knowledgeable planning through consultations with the public is well understood.

I have pointed to the intranet operating network as the communication tool for many reasons. The intranet has been used for internal communication, transferring data internally (internal IPs) the same way the Internet does it externally (external IPs). It is the presence of safety features that make the

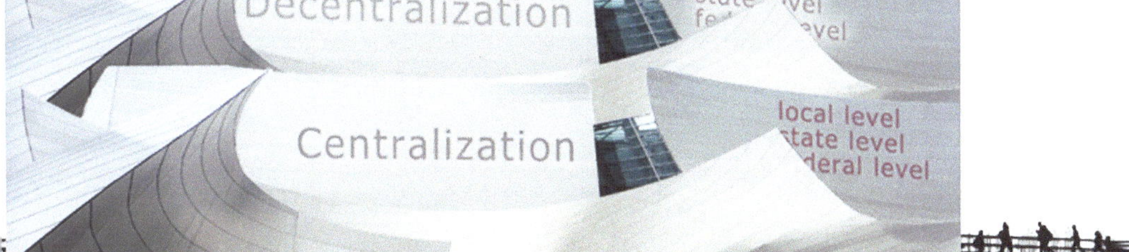

intranet the viable choice for keeping operational data. Internal IPs are critical for validation and processing data contents.

We may even go so far as to say that with the intranet as a public tool in operation, the Internet should become less of a target and have fewer incentives for malicious activity. The network in operation enables the public and the administration to act pragmatically as partners, giving the public agenda the exposure needed for orientation and participatory competence. That's a desirable scenario. Political menus are not commonly known for offering public dishes. The perspective of public policies pursued in an adequate political model can confuse even advanced social thinkers.

The concept of participatory democracy avoids the limitations of indirect democracy. I will ignore false truisms, such as, "We need better people working for us in the government." Even great people on the wrong train will not get to the right destination. With technological advances turned into social tooling, the societies will gain their services optimized for quality.

one account missed on your desktop:
your municipal citizen account

6 ECONOMIC DIVERSITY

Socialism is known for its bad side of practicing political suppression of the private sector and capitalism should be recognized for practicing political suppression of the public sector. Having a robust economy is everyone's business, but paradoxically 80% or so is busy servicing the reaming portion.

Before, I believed in the power of arguments; the selectively developed society to me looked like a body of unified consciousness in need of pursuing many goals that reflected its characters. There are plenty of poor people reading business sections, and many rich ones reading the dissident press, indicating the need for practical assistance to this mental displacement.

The human consciousness needs to operate without modifying it from outside. Communities can advance without preconditions exclusively by getting relevant knowledge on supported, joint network – publicly financed.

Whether it's the private business, the local cooperative or the promoted municipal entity, political support for each type requires dedicated services. The output is political, but the input depends on generating communal support representing the need for an integrated system of public–administration communication and operating on specific orientations.

This part of the book extends into areas that are known, but due to the dominating interest being the loudest of them all, they are known from a different angle. Our political orientations manifest our economic beliefs. Those orientations remain in a pre-coordinated stage.

Wall Street and Hedge Funds are known more for their financial stands then for their collective efforts to gain dominance in investing and profit. Building up orientation in the inner-working of local economies gives collective municipality as well as other local players better chance to face economic challenges by consolidating their act.

The joint network helps in being on the same page organizationally. We use to think of the economy rule, as a one-fits-all method. That's the reason why small businesses are not integrating, that's the reason that the otherwise attractive cooperatives are the small portion of the economic landscape. Further, the economic interest of the communal municipality is another reason the one-size-fits-all economy is a candidate for verification. By presenting the municipal one-share per local citizen model we may be embarking on a concept balancing the big picture in advanced development.

I should bring to attention the most neglected and least understood area: public ownership. We all as private citizens have a vital interest in it. Ownership is never symbolic, regardless of the sector of operation. Public properties have been handled differently by authorities, from splendid development to quiet sellout. Public wealth proved to be an easy target. Leaving its symbolism behind, public ownership moves into actual ownership by the voters' support.

Autonomous practices of local economic sectors would enforce their simultaneous development. A pragmatically designed public ownership to benefit citizenry through non-transferable [(non-speculative) shares is the most obvious candidate for a comprehensive public ownership model. Such an arrangement best represents assets branded as "belonging to all."

A scenario: Each generation gets their equal, non-transferable share, regulated by general policy ratifications. This concept is to organize and maintain the scope of public assets through generations, directly involving the community's economic stand. Will this limit the private and coop operations locally? Just the opposite. The changes in market demand create market opportunities.

The present economic model thou using two productive sectors: private and public – divides them economically. Only one creates value. Where is the value of the other sector?

Moving chunks of the public sector into municipal operations owned collectively, the market gains the value of operation in the amount of being transferred.

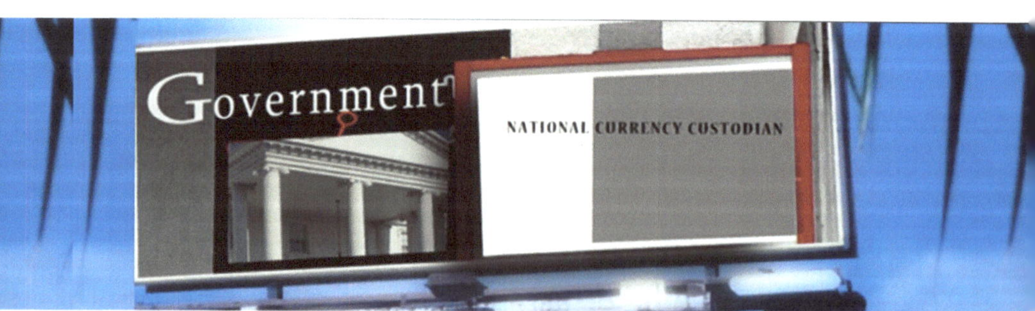

Political participation is what links work with the wealth. I must be getting too futuristic. It is not getting any less futuristic to touch on some of the trends underlying politics related to the economy. To withstand the argument that money is only topics for those who have the former, we should ask ourselves what a democracy is for. Because the economic equation is the product of political blueprints, there is no better option for society at large than injecting itself into the midst of the business to gain representation as the political clout. It has been counterproductive to argue outside politics.

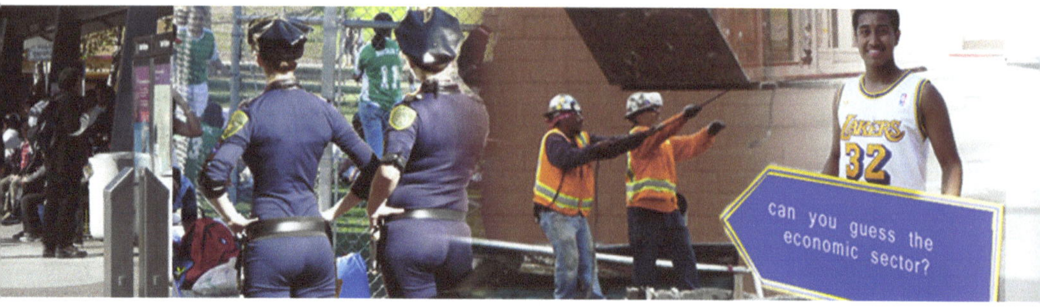

7 TAXATION PARADOX

Taxes are ideologically most entrenched myth of the economy, affecting a mind-blowing portion of human activities. With all their associated concerns, they are not what they appear to be. More often than not –paradoxically – taxes serve those who oppose them as a buffer against public sector operating as the missing leg of an economy. Taxation is misconstrued by those who support it by justifying them as a means to finance basic services. Taxes were introduced to control the growth of economy long before any democratic processes surfaced, but they remain as the irresistible source of cash. Note: today's monopolized economy have thirst for direct monetary extraction. The role taxes play requires some explanations which must remain futile as long as public sectors remain on welfare.

We have bought into the scenario of huge debts payments and small services performed with resources obtained from mandating other sources to pay for it. The proponents' question follows: "But who will pay for all those services?" The question ought to be, "Where is the direct market value of those services being counted?" The bigger the scope of public services, the bigger their market value; therefore, the greater the public sector's needs, the more financial drawback is required to fulfill them. Call this perpetual development-deficiency syndrome. Suppressed accounting causes money shortages in circulation that affect the economic balance. By this arrangement, the market demand is systematically reduced. Increase in production (also the sale) of one item leads to a decrease (the sale) in another with no link of market productivity to the amount of spending money. Taxation may have a strong anti-inflationary quality (two jobs for the price of one), but it undermines income per capita. The market lacks accounting for the value of products and services in the public sector and undercuts the private one.

How do the economic books add up? Borrowing money for work that will be paid back with money taken from other work is almost as complicated as it is costly. Einstein once said, "The hardest thing in the world to understand is income tax." He may be too kind. Overall, taxation reduces the market with the amount being taxed.

Politics is a business, which comes down to whose business it is. Allowing the work of both sectors to practice the same accounting would add value, not subtract it from the balance sheet. This can be done by booking municipality under citizen's equal-ownership program of the respective locations. It would indicate a broader part of the economy active, and at the same time put the economic books on the path out of the red.

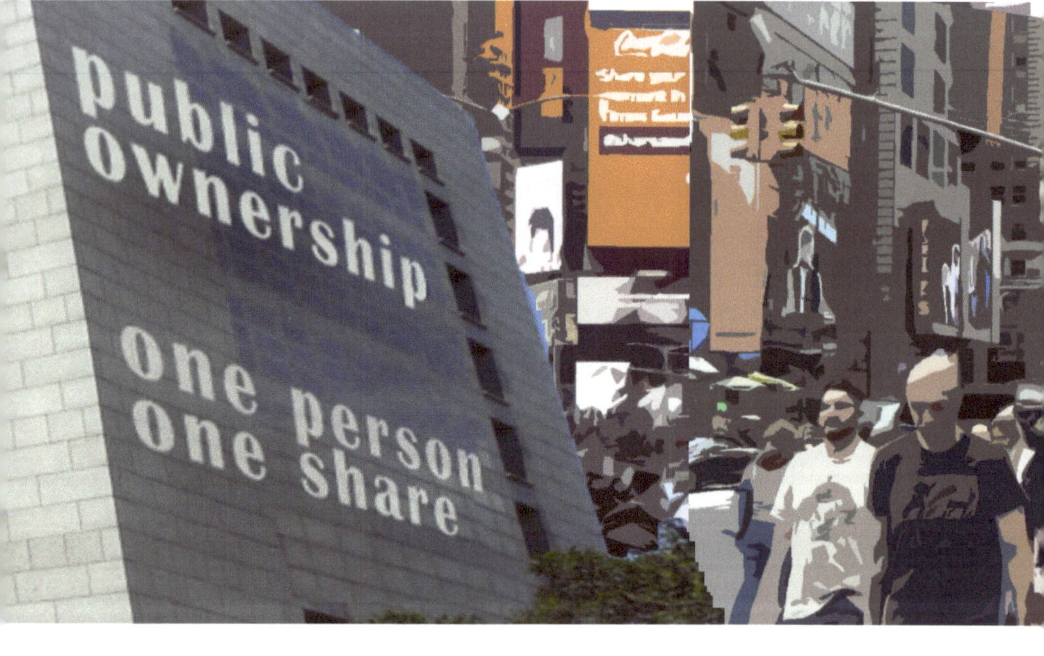
public
ownership

one person
one share

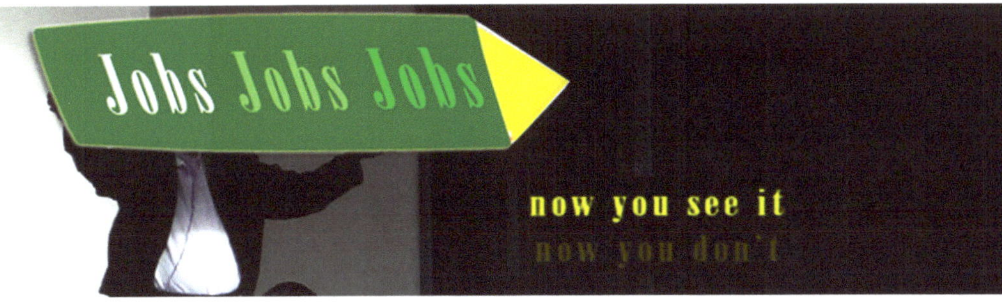

8 JOBS JOBS JOBS

One particular aspect of the jobs is as enigmatic as the logic of taxation. They are being booked as a cost to businesses, which means they are recorded as the cost to the economy. This implies that people themselves remain outside their economic calculations. Lower labor cost correlates with the higher economy. It is the other way around when we don't examine economics but the standard of living it produces. Are we living in The Twilight Zone?

It is not the role of the employers to raise their cost. It is the business of employees to raise their value of work for the services. Likewise, separating geographically the markets of production and consumption couldn't take into account the social ramification because it is the job of politicians to represent the interest of those who voted for them—the working population. Tariffs were used in times of building nations. Once they were abolished by internationalizing the profits, the domestic audience was exposed to the consequences. What this has to do with the Municipal Citizen Accounts? You don't oppose the enormous successes of the global economy. You become its partner regionally, by building a community based on political power withstanding the economic demands.

The one-share per citizen project of municipality's assets and operation is not limited to remedying socioeconomic imbalances. Any public institution needs a think-tank as much as the other foundations do. The arrangements are different for non-hierarchical settings. Existing cases of cryptocurrency have no public oversight and are not suitable for community practices. It would be well justified for the think tanks to create a veritable model.

Well-to-do society ought to prioritize the citizen involvement in all aspect not covered in economies pertaining to social financing, renewable energy or landscaping inhabited areas. Note: The sail-ships designers were champions of harvesting the wind power, and hydro-energy plants designers were the champions of turbine designs. The social planners commissioned the wind farms to have steep learning. The ecology potentially adding its value to the economy, not dragging it down, should not be a pipe dream either.

first comes evaluation

then comes theory how this came to be

then, was there anything used to prevent it

than, if so why it didn't work

and finally, is there any alternative that hasn't been used before

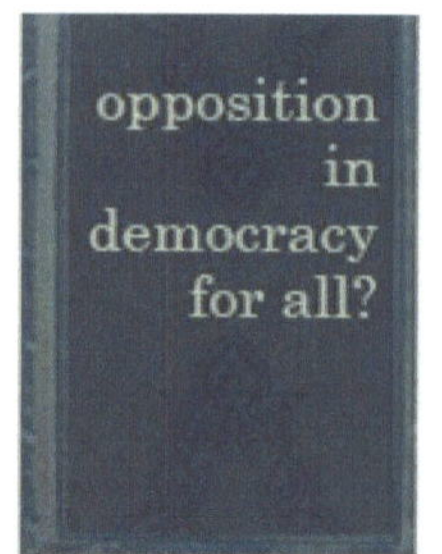

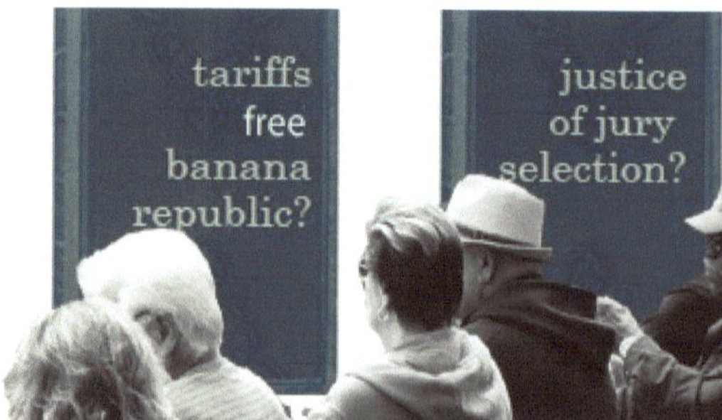

9 STIMULUS-SIDE RETIREMENT

The form of the supply-side economics is political. The market is exposed to two opposite trends. To increase the production to increase profit, or to boost prices to do the same. The role of responsive politics is to promote the first trend and suppress the other by using simple methods. The money in circulation has vaporizing tendencies. Supply side economy partially remedies the problem. Examining one basic commonality of interest leads us to the topic of financial security at post-productive age.

Social Security comes to mind as the best candidate for an economic stimulus factor to be considered, guaranteeing every generation an adequate social standard during retirement. The burden on young and older people's paychecks could be unnecessary if sound money circulation is introduced.

With raising awareness of linking standard of living to politics, many unobtainable goals gain viability. The range of opportunities is attached to the level of integration. The Social Security arena has such a gigantic scope that only broad political coordination can address it.

To be or not to be a stable society is always a democracy-leading question. The prospect for bringing a stimulus-side retirement for public approval or disapproval lies down the future road of self-determination. Social Security could become then a significant catalyst. Again, it would take the government acting as the monetary system custodian. "The veterans of the labor force and professionals have been giving their lives to erect wealth for others, and are perfectly capable, as the seniors – to contribute to potent economic undertakings as the rightful agents of economic stimulus.

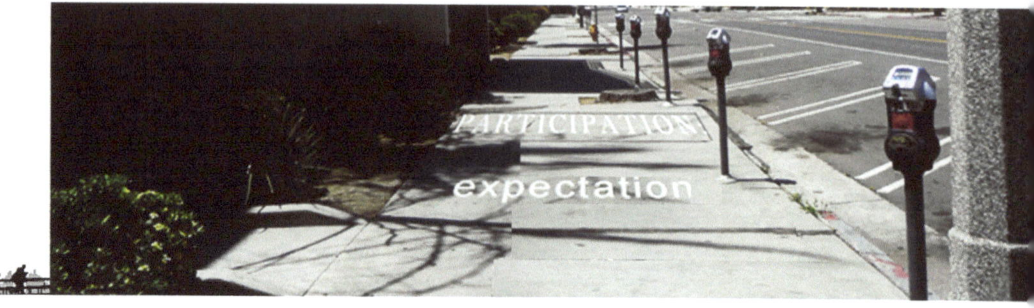

10 WORK-BASED DEVELOPMENT

Thinking big is the product of opportunities. The social aspects of life are best addressed not as service, but staging a direct involvement. Unrestrained logic maintains utopia. Let us summarize a few things that do not match the common narratives:

— The government's activity ignores the value of public work involved, substituting it with taxation.
— The arbitrary wages on the market lock its value mechanism.
— Unproductive jobs, including involuntary unemployment, vastly raise the cost to the economy
— Small businesses lack the ability to integrate or merge.
— Cooperatives lack political support.
— Banking activities outside public involvement contribute to money supply imbalance.
— Interest rates act as arbitrary taxation system, adding to the cost of the official one.
— Stock market dominance hampers the prospect of a broad based economy

In keeping our eyes on the ball, however, we must restrain ourselves from an overly critical inclination. Due to the distinctive characteristics the public and private sectors possess, they can complement each other, giving society more options in a less restrictive setting. So what would be the central piece of the well-to-do, work-value attributed society? The answer: creating local legislation shaped through public ratification. This allows every new generation maintaining social continuum. It has everything to do with political options linked with individual access.

In the grand perspective, though the pace of societal development depends on society's place in the flow of legislative initiatives on all administrative levels. The capacity to reinvest the accumulated capital, to eradicate interest rates and taxes not authorized by society are among the conditions. As different societal groups have different outlooks on economic relations, we can expect the emergence of choices for future generations. Here are some examples of futuristic views in socioeconomic development:

(a) Government being a national currency custodian in the role of the lender, having branches for banks in all sectors.

(b) Currency volume in circulation reflects the value of products and services on the market (classic economy).

(c) Monopoly-free environment replacing regulations with choices (except for environmental and public health hazard issues).

(d) Ownership types having political representation.

(e) Anti-inflationary programs targeting price spiking occurrences with broad production credits.

How long is the waiting line we do not know.

subconscious mind fed by unfavorable circumstances
is able to operate in a cooperative mode

11 DEMOCRATIC PURPOSE

People habitually express their views. Some when asked, some without asking. Some views are monitored for marketing and security purposes without knowledge and consent. One of the off base political reinforcement is to label people as a political minority. Having the entire society politically active is not a metaphorical proposition. Is there a way to evaluate such an assumption? No, the conflicting term "opposition" proves the democracy's drawback by going halfway – maintaining the systemic exclusion. Managing most of the available to vote population without representation cannot be accidental. What are the political attributes of majority and minority? They float back and forth from election to election without a clear purpose.

Having municipal accounts by voters sounds big but needs realistic implementation. If the statement "Those who are organized are much better off than those who are not" is true, as we know it is, what purpose is there in keeping voters unorganized for integrating them with a capable administration? That said, let's not be enigmatic any more than the uncharted territory imposes.

Should the idea of network-based public-government interactions be the elephant in the room? Society cooperation could hardly take place without methodical communication. The elections' wins and losses have no tangible results in it. When assimilation and adaptation skills are the dominating factors, a big chunk of community expansion is missing. The far-reaching "municipal supplement to the economy in form of equal shares to GDP" concept will do away with the winners- takes-all "pastiche" of democratic principles – also with people's migration for economic reasons.

What is missing? Appropriate incentives for representatives and candidates to develop public input and two-way communication. I say: overcoming the existing disconnect. Autonomies cure conflicts of interests, as they open doors that are locked. Pre-agreements take place among two or more sides. The sides are the community's trends and orientations emerging on the public network. It is the advantage of local environments, free from the national responsibility of maintaining foreign policy and security issues.

Under the free flow of municipal information, the benefits of consensuses among valid interests will lead to bigger roles for local parties who attract by accessibility, transparency, and participatory decision making. With the population in active mode, the role of political partics arc mutually strengthened.

The majority-minority window dressing – ignoring the elementary requirement of post-election development – is immobilizing. The public's bigger role in own affairs suggests electoral choices matched with orientation, allowing parties to operate under one umbrella before and after an election—without polarization.

The idea here is to have mechanisms to remove roadblocks when they appear. The unified purpose to obtain such mechanism takes pre-agreements for a model. Pragmatism attracting participation is synonymous with the support of legislative market featuring ratification. It is so when offers are written for all the audience. Once candidates for office bring the network-based participatory concepts to the table, the life will begin gaining colors.

Although we are a broad crowd of many orientations, we may find more commonality among ourselves than acknowledged. With opportunity knocking, we will find that we are not all that different while local administrative branches are accessible to the voters' contact points and legislative curtains remain open, especially, while the processes of public ratification of local legislation ensure the public way.

12 INFORMATIVE ENGINE

Our political subconscious involuntarily reacts to given rules in a competitive mode, keeping the voter struggling for unobtainable goals. Privilege emboldened by omnipresent hierarchy dressed in democratic feathers obfuscates political cooperation. The topic of autonomy is muted. Should I bring a historical perspective? Replacing one privileged option with another didn't stop the chain of revolutions. Had the autonomy been implemented, no revolution would ever take place. The level of public discontent seems to fluctuate but grow exponentially in time.

What allows culture to evolve is information. The absence of attractive, marketable item like publicly-ran for sustainable trends in socio-economic development through direct democracy is perhaps due to the absence of public interest in available information. Any movement aimed at populist support must have an information structure in place that builds on data created by members. Only the administration is capable of taking the role of a host.

Evaluation of the contemporary results of public actions are omitted and not followed by the organizers. The cause of public-governments integration doesn't advance because the public and the government have no platform to communicate. Local administrations supporting the network and public data channels will fill the gap.

If a character was stronger than money, the political class would not need the incentives of the latter. It is the lack of correct motivations and the presence of wrong ones that keep societies and governments apart.

Progress is a matter of evolving information. Professionally handling diverse trends requires diverse knowledge. Who other than the voters themselves would support processes leading to political experience? Who can be more interested in supporting voters' oriented issues? One thing leads to another. Democratic processes that have traditionally been kept out of the spotlight – as I have argued – can only evolve through voter-centered information channels on the dedicated network. Managing the voters' accounts is managing the necessary content of growth-oriented information.

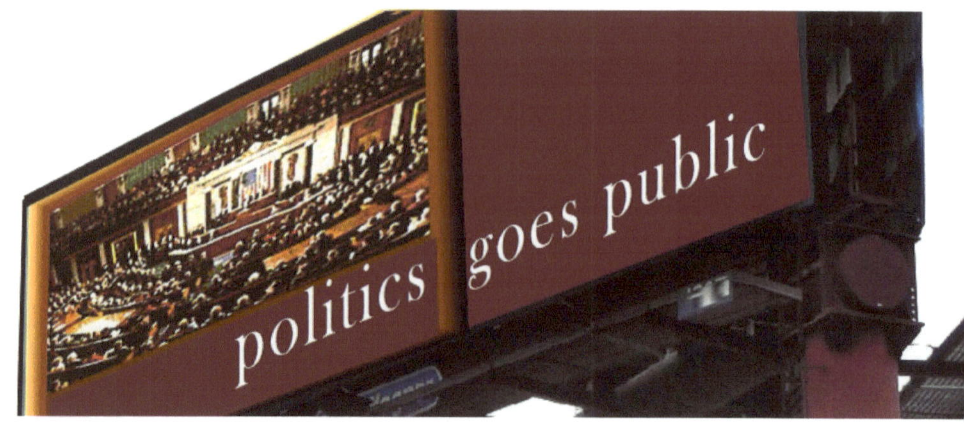

13 THE COMMON SPRINGBOARD

Have private beaches, lakes, forests or banks something to do with exclusion? The consensus is that the existing voting routines have outlived their usefulness due to lack of impact on the course of events. Yet another consensus ought to be added: acknowledging that democracy can extend its effectiveness and better pinpoint its post-election objectives.
So how close are we to the concept of a far-reaching autonomy for significant trends in politics? Let us see what we have:
The political accounts? Not yet.
The interconnectivity? Not yet.
The pre-agreements? Not yet.
The administrative data generated by the source—the voter? Not yet.
The public ratifications? Not yet.
The grassroots-oriented political parties specializing in electronic democracy? Not yet.

Public sphere can thrive optimally on public grounds. Is the local administration the public ground? Can the administration facilitate the space? We should concentrate on candidates and representatives working on this potential.

Evaluating and fascinating community trends is the supporters' prerogative. The representatives will gain the orientation based on the communication.

We have gone beyond the concept of a transparent and open to petition government, to further emphasize the core issue of the voter's place at the table. The one-step solution presented could hardly convince anyone if such a step were not self-explanatory. It means that the concept of boosting the voters' range of operations from electing public officials to ratifying local legislation is challenging but understandable. The citizen network as the one-step solution is characterized by the following:

(a) local hi-fi intranet network (personal IPs)

(b) voters–administration communication system

(c) public database (integrated public input)

(d) decentralized public–government information channels of interests

What I hope stays with the reader is the realization that decentralization of decision-making on all levels of administration (though only the local level is the proper one for individuals being 'plugged-in') is the answer. The new tools of social coexistence are more than a promise of greater perspectives. Having the wants requires having the means.

Would you not say that guided by right incentives, all the right intentions have room for falling into place? It is hard to offer a more attractive program for an aspiring politician than having a voter-oriented network in formal and informal operations. Progress has always relied on people opening new doors to popular demands. An active society, however, amounts to the number of votes as the political currency to maintain their course.

The concept of electronic participation locally may not have a smooth ride. But it will prevail just as the voting rights are continually evolving, to make making changes in this world tilt toward the public. As this book proclaims, the means to obtain a place at the table is more realistic that some want to believe.

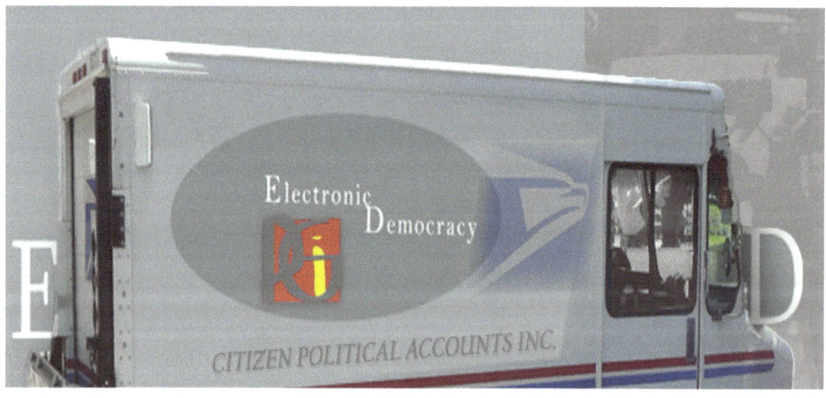

THE GRAND HOPE

The pyramids have overshadowed
    slaves who build them
    The slaves tried copying the masters
    ever since
    Today the Neverland looks less colorful
    than ever
    and the Savior cannot show you the way

When millions awake to each other
to build the space for themselves

    where will all this lead us?

. . . we will not know, till then.

 *Author's Note*

How futuristic this endeavor may be is determined by the faith of the direct democracy staging itself in the waiting line.

The Pharaoh's era of elephants building pyramid graves lasted thousands of year. With the consecutive social experiments gradually improving in time, the direct democracy may arrive in the time-span of one generation: in the name of harvesting the content of human consciousness.

Thanks, Edward W.

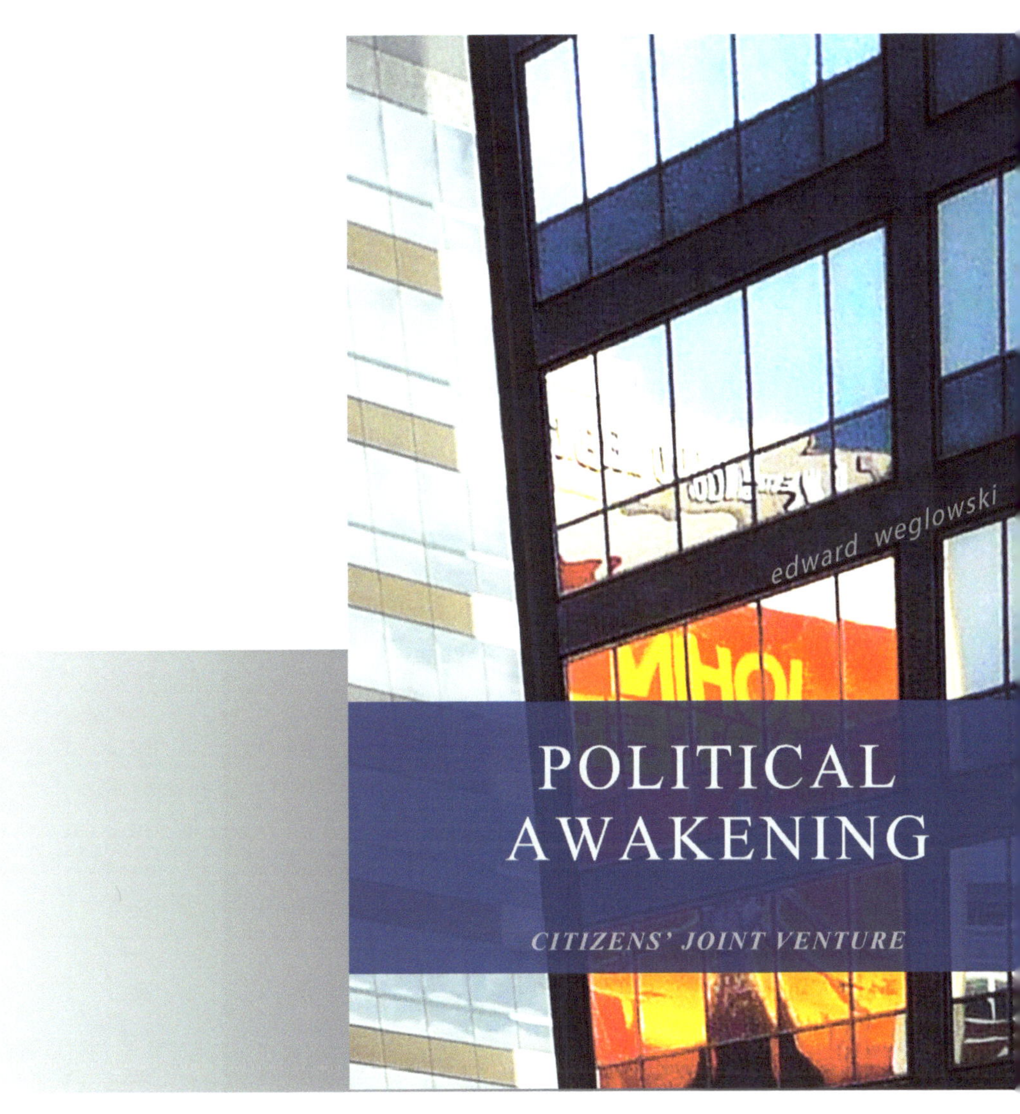

close-up to unified social theory